Still More Legends of the Elders

by

John W. Friesen Ph.D., D.Min., D.R.S.

and

Virginia Lyons Friesen Ph. D.

Illustrations by David J Friesen B. Ed.

DETSELIG
ENTERPRISES LTD

Still More Legends of the Elders

© 2004 John W. Friesen and Virginia Lyons Friesen

National Library of Canada Cataloguing in Publication

Friesen, John W.
   Still more legends of the elders / John W. Friesen &
Virginia Lyons Friesen.

ISBN 1-55059-279-3

   1. Indians of North America–Folklore. 2.Legends–North
America. I.Friesen, Virginia Agnes Lyons, II. Title.

E98.F6F744 2005   398.2'089'97   C2004-906816-4

We acknowledge the support of the Government of Canada through the Book Publishing Industry Development
Program (BPIDP) for our publishing program.

We also acknowledge the support of the Alberta Founda-
tion for the Arts for our publishing program.

COMMITTED TO THE DEVELOPMENT OF CULTURE AND THE ARTS

Detselig Enterprises Ltd.
210 - 1220 Kensington Rd NW
Calgary, Alberta T2N 3P5
Telephone: 403-283-0900
Fax: 403-283-6947
Email: temeron@telusplanet.net
www.temerondetselig.com

SAN. 113-0234
ISBN 1-55059-279-3
Printed in Canada

Cover design by Alvin Choong

Table of Contents

To the memory of the late
Alva Townsend Snow,
Quechen First Nation Yuma, AZ

The Significance of Indian Legends

Welcome to the third volume of this series offering still more legends of the elders. Legends have sometimes been identified as one of the most common means of transmitting First Nations cultural values and beliefs. There was a time when all cultures relied solely on the oral tradition and there were no written forms of communication. Legends or stories that were shared between families and communities conveyed important belief systems, ceremonial rituals, and cultural symbols. Aboriginal bands specialized in the use of this medium.

This generation of Canadians and Americans is very fortunate in being able to access Native legends. Appreciation for the preservation of these tales must be extended to several sectors, particularly elders who through the years have taken upon themselves the responsibility of maintaining the essence of the oral tradition during times when their people were under siege to abandon traditional ways. These guardians of revered knowledge have been successful in keeping many of their valued beliefs and practices alive through very turbulent times. Adherents to the written word who first came into contact with Indigenous cultures, such as traders, missionaries, and anthropologists also rendered a valuable service by committing to writing many stories they learned from their new found acquaintances.

Native legends have a unique identity. They are truly Indigenous stories, and as such they constitute the oral literature of each particular tribal cultural configuration. Indian stories are pictures of Aboriginal life verbally drawn by Indigenous artists, showing life from their point of view. Legends deal with spirituality, the origins of things, and various kinds of individual behavior. Legends are often entertaining and they may convey a vast range of cultural knowledge including folkways, values and beliefs. Legends often outline the very basis of a particular cultural pattern. The sacred number four is referred to in several of the legends.

The study of Native legends can be a very rich source of learning. Traditionally, legends appear to have been told for a variety of purposes, both formal and informal. Formal storytelling was usually connected to the occasion of deliberate moral or spiritual instruction. In fact, some legends were considered so sacred or special that their telling was restricted to the celebration of a very special event such as the Sundance. Others were told only during specific seasons. On these occasions, only recognized or designated persons could engage in their telling. Nearly anyone could engage in informal storytelling, and such legends were usually shared for their entertainment or instructional value.

It is possible to classify Indian legends into four categories (with some degree of overlap), each of which has a special purpose. The four types of legends are as follows.

(i) Entertainment legends are often about the trickster, who is called by different names among the various tribes. For example, the Blackfoot call him Napi, the Crees call him Wisakedjak, the Ojibway call him Nanabush, the Sioux call him îktômni, and other tribes have different names for him like Coyote, Tarantula, or Raven. Stories about the trickster are principally fictional and can be invented and amended even during the process of storytelling.

Trickster stories often involve playing tricks. Sometimes the trickster plays tricks on others and sometimes they play tricks on him. The trickster appears to have the advantage on his unsuspecting audience, however, since he possesses supernatural powers, which he deploys on a whim to startle or to shock. He has powers to raise animals to life and he himself may even die and in four days come to life again. Aside from being amusing, trickster stories often incorporate knowledge about aspects of Aboriginal culture such as buffalo hunts, natural phenomena, rituals, or the relationship between people and animals. In this sense trickster stories could also be instructional.

(ii) Instructional or teaching legends are basically told for the purpose of sharing information about a tribe's culture, history, or origin. These stories often use animal motifs to explain why things are the way they are. A child may enquire about the origin of the seasons or the creation of the world and a tale about animal life may be told. For example, a child may ask, "Where did our people come from?" or "Why are crows' feathers black?" Stories told in response to these questions could include adventures of the trickster.

(iii) Moral legends are intended to teach ideal or "right" forms of behavior, and are employed to suggest to the listener that a change in attitude or action would be desirable. Since traditional Indian tribes rarely corporally punished their children they sometimes found it useful to hint at the inappropriateness of certain behavior by telling stories. For example, the story might be about an animal that engages in inappropriate behavior and the child is supposed to realize that a possible modification of his or her own behavior is the object of the telling.

(iv) Sacred or spiritual legends can be told only by a recognized elder or other tribal approved individual and their telling is considered a form of worship. That tradition is respected in this volume so there are no sacred legends included.

In traditional times, spiritually significant stories were never told to just anyone who asked. Nor were they told by just anyone. In some tribes, sacred legends were considered property and thus their transmission from generation to generation was carefully safeguarded. Selected individuals learned a legend by careful listening; then, on mastering the story, passed it on to succeeding generations, perhaps changing aspects of the story to suit their own tastes. The amendments would center on a different choice of animals or sites referred to in the story and preferred by the teller.

Legends comprised only a part of a tribe's spiritual structure, which also included ceremonies, rituals, songs, and dances. Physical objects such as fetishes, pipes, painted tepee designs, medicine bundles, and shrines of sorts, supplemented these. Familiarity with these components comprised sacred knowledge, and everything learned was committed to memory. Viewed together these entries represent spiritual connections between people and the universe which, with appropriate care, resulted in a lifestyle of assured food supply, physical well-being, and satisfying the needs and wants of the society and its members.

The stories contained in this volume have been drawn from many different sources including fieldwork, personal contact, reading, and anthropological studies. Through the years we have visited most of the tribes represented in this book, and have taught university courses in First Nations communities including Blackfoot, Chipewyan, Cree, Stoney (Nakoda Sioux), and Tsuu T'ina (Sarcee). Each legend in this book originated with a different First Nation, although there is some overlap. For further information, a glossary is available in the teacher's handbook.

The essence of each story contained in this volume has been preserved although the legends have been shortened and written in language that may readily be understood by children. This volume is dedicated to the reality that one cannot value too highly the importance of Indian legends. Through this means students of Aboriginal ways can learn a great deal about Indian philosophy and, hopefully, increase respect for their ways.

Trickster Legends

Coyote and Crow
A Yakima Legend

One day Coyote (the trickster) traveled to the Pacific coast where the rivers and lakes were full of fish. When he arrived at his destination he was weary and very hungry. In fact, Coyote was so tired that he did not even feel like putting a net into the water to catch fish. He lay down beneath a tree and immediately fell asleep.

When the trickster awoke he saw Crow sitting on the branch of a tree high above him. Crow had his mouth full of fish and seeing the fish made Coyote even hungrier. He decided to get the fish from Crow, one way or another.

"Hello Crow," he shouted. "I am happy to meet you. I have heard a great deal about you. They tell me that you have a wonderful voice and I have come a long way to hear it. Please, say something to me. Better still; why not sing a song for me? I would like to hear you sing."

Crow did not want to open his mouth because the fish he was holding in his mouth would fall, so he made a quiet muffled noise.

"What is that sound you are making?" Coyote questioned. "I am a little deaf and cannot hear you. I would like to hear you sing. Please sing for me."

It is hard to sing with something in your mouth and Crow knew it. He wanted very much to eat the fish he had in his mouth so again he made a quiet noise while continuing to hold the fish in his mouth. Coyote tried a third time to make Crow sing. Crow only made a humming noise and held onto the fish he had in his mouth.

Coyote grew impatient. It was taking too long to get Crow to open his mouth, and Coyote kept getting hungrier. He tried a fourth time.

"Crow," he said. "Just this morning I heard that the animals want to make you chief. They sent me to tell you the good news." Crow was so surprised that in spite of himself his mouth fell open in amazement. As it did the fish dropped straight down, right into Coyote's waiting mouth.

"Thank you for the food, you silly Crow," Coyote shouted. He was really going to enjoy himself. He told Crow, "The next time someone flatters you, don't pay so much attention. Now go about your foolishness and let me enjoy my meal."

Crow learned a valuable lesson that day.

Coyote and Spider
A Mohawk Legend

It was winter, and there was ice and snow everywhere. Coyote was very cold. He had not bothered gathering wood for his fire and there was no food in his house. He had planned to sing a special winter song to make sure that it would be a mild winter, but he had forgotten to do so. Now it was too late. This was indeed a very fierce winter.

Instead of getting ready for winter, Coyote had spent his time watching Spider weaving his web across his window. Coyote was fascinated with weaving, and every move Spider made was a real work of art. Spider saw that Coyote was watching him so he really decided to show off. Every strand of his web was beautifully strung and Coyote sat spellbound. "I can learn so much by watching this," said Coyote.

Spider thought that if Coyote would keep watching and do nothing else, he would eventually get so hungry and weak that Spider could make Coyote into his slave. Everything was going according to plan when Coyote's cousin, Red Fox, suddenly showed up. Immediately Red Fox saw what Spider was up to and decided to stop him. He felt sorry for Coyote and wanted to help him.

"Your house is very cold," he told Coyote, but Coyote paid no attention and kept on watching Spider. Red Fox went outside to gather firewood and find some food. He built a roaring fire, cooked some food and offered it to Coyote. Coyote pushed the food away saying, "I am learning a great deal by watching Spider. Please leave me alone."

Red Fox would not give up. He grabbed Spider's web from the window and threw it on the ground. Now Coyote could look out of his window and see the clear blue sky outside. It was all very beautiful and he felt very much awake. He suddenly realized what had happened.

"That tricky Spider had me in a spell," he said. "Thank you for pulling me out of it. I am hungry now and I want to eat." Quickly he gulped down the supper that Red Fox had made and snuggled up to the fire for a long, long nap.

Red Fox and Coyote remained very good friends after that.

Raven Builds a Canoe
A Flathead Legend

As Raven, the trickster, was traveling along one day he grew very hungry. He had not eaten for several days. Suddenly he noticed a little house in the woods where a widow and her daughter Red Bird, lived. The widow invited Raven inside and gave him a delicious supper. Raven noticed that there was plenty of food around so he decided to stay for a while.

Raven observed that Red Bird was very beautiful and she would make a good wife. Besides, he liked the fact that there was plenty of food in the lodge. He asked the widow if he could marry Red Bird. The widow was pleased that Raven wanted to marry her daughter. "It would be good to have a man around the house," she said. Unfortunately, Raven had good meals on his mind, not marriage.

A few days after the wedding, Raven announced to Red Bird that he was going to build a canoe for her mother. "She should have a canoe of her own," said Raven. This made Red Bird very happy. She told her mother about Raven's plans, and her mother got very excited. It would indeed be a very fine thing to own a canoe.

Raven went off into the woods to find just the right cedar tree from which to build the canoe. At the end of the day he came back to the house and told Red Bird that he had found just the perfect tree. His mother-in-law was so happy that she cooked a huge meal for Raven. After eating supper, Raven announced that the next morning he would cut down the tree out of which he would build the canoe. Then he laid down for a nap.

When Raven woke up he ate a big breakfast and headed for the woods. Soon Red Bird and her mother heard the sound of the crashing of a tree in the distance. They thought Raven must have cut down the tree. "I am so happy," said Red Bird's mother. "Finally I will have a canoe of my own with which to travel."

When Raven came home that night he told Red Bird that he preferred to have salmon soup to eat each evening after a hard day's work. He said it would not be long and the three of them would be taking a long canoe ride down the river. Red Bird told her mother to prepare salmon soup for Raven each night. He needed to be strong because of the hard work he was doing.

On the fourth day, Red Bird's mother could not wait any longer. She told Red Bird secretly to follow Raven into the woods. She wanted to know just how the work was progressing on the canoe. Red Bird did as she was told and followed her husband into the woods. She walked very quietly so that Raven would not hear her. What she saw astonished her. Raven was standing next to a rotten old tree that was lying on the ground, and his axe made a chopping sound as he hit the dead tree stump. He had not cut down a cedar tree after all. He was not building a canoe. He was only pretending.

Red Bird ran home quickly and told her mother what she had seen. The two of them gathered up their things and left quickly for a nearby village. All they left behind were some empty bags and the ashes of a fire.

When Raven came home that night all he found was an empty house. Now he realized that he had fooled no one and again he had nothing to eat. He started walking to his next adventure.

Trickster and the Sun
A Cheyenne Legend

A long time ago, Sun had a pair of beautiful leggings that allowed him to work miracles. Veeho (the trickster) greatly admired them. One day Veeho visited Sun and when Sun was not looking, Veeho stole the leggings. "Aha," he chortled. "Now I have the magic leggings and I will be able to work wonders."

The trickster ran away from Sun. He travelled all day and all night and eventually grew very tired. As he lay down to rest, he rolled up the leggings and used them for his pillow. When he woke in the morning he found himself back in Sun's lodge. Veeho had forgotten that Sun travels all around the earth and sees everything.

"What are you doing with my leggings?" Sun asked the trickster. Of course because Veeho was the trickster, he had a ready answer. "I needed a pillow to sleep on so I borrowed your leggings," he said slyly. "I knew you wouldn't mind." Sun pretended to believe the trickster, but he knew Veeho was not telling the truth.

"Well, I must be off on my morning walk," said Sun. "Take care of my lodge for me while I am gone." Veeho agreed, and as soon as Sun was out of sight, the trickster again ran off with Sun's leggings. This time he ran twice as far as he had before, but he was so tired he had to stop to sleep. When he awoke he found himself back in Sun's lodge again.

Sun laughed when the trickster woke up. "If you are so fond of my leggings that you have to steal them," he told Veeho, "go ahead and keep them. Let's pretend we are having a giveaway feast and I just gave you the leggings."

Veeho insisted that he was only playing a trick on Sun but he was very happy to keep the leggings. He quickly put on the leggings and left Sun's lodge as fast as he could. He decided to try out the magic of the leggings. He started a prairie fire with them that would drive the buffalo toward him. That way he would not have to go hunting for buffalo.

Unfortunately, Veeho did not have Sun's power and he could not handle the huge fire he had started. The fire came toward him so fast that it scorched his leggings and ruined them. Soon the leggings were burned to a crisp. The trickster begged Sun for another pair of leggings but Sun refused. "You had your chance," said Sun. "Next time you need to be more careful."

And so Veeho, the trickster, learned another lesson.

Coyote and Little Snake
A Wichita Legend

It was a bright sunny day and Coyote (the trickster) was walking along feeling wicked. He felt like playing a trick on someone. Whoever he met as he walked along would be in for a surprise.

Suddenly Coyote saw a tiny snake wriggling along beside his feet. At first he felt a little bit sorry for the snake because it was so tiny, but he decided to have fun with the snake anyway. Coyote was in a wicked mood.

"Say there, Little Snake," he said. "What is life like down there on the ground? It must be very difficult to live so close to the ground. Someone could come along and step on you any time." Little Snake did not say much but kept on wriggling along on the ground. Coyote spoke again.

"I guess there is not much good in being a little snake, is there?" the trickster teased. Let us play a little game with each another," he challenged. "Let us bite one another and see what happens."

Much to Coyote's surprise, Little Snake agreed to play the game. Coyote knew he could bite harder than Little Snake.

So Little Snake bit Coyote and Coyote hardly felt it. It was a very small bite. When it was Coyote's turn he bit Little Snake extra hard, so hard, in fact, that Little Snake could not crawl anymore. It was evident that Little Snake was in great pain. Coyote went off feeling quite smug.

As the trickster walked along he suddenly began to feel weak. The further he walked, the weaker he got. Finally, he could walk no more and he lay down to rest. He was feeling very sick and began to feel that he was going to die. He realized that the snake bite was making him sick.

Coyote probably would have died if his cousin Red Fox had not come along with some medicine to save him.

In the meantime Little Snake's wound healed, and he wriggled off. Soon he came upon Coyote lying on the ground. Little Snake said to Coyote; "Sometimes it is not the size of bite that matters. It is what is in the bite that counts."

Coyote learned a valuable lesson that day.

Swift-Runner and the Trickster
A Zuni Legend

In the beginning there was only one tarantula on earth who was the trickster. Every morning when Tarantula was getting up he heard the footsteps of a young Zuni warrior running past his house. The warrior's name was Swift-Runner, and he was always dressed in his ceremonial clothing when he took his morning run.

One morning Tarantula stopped Swift-Runner on his run. "Say there," said the trickster. "I like your fine clothes."

"Thank you," said Swift-Runner, "but I must continue my run. I have a long way to go before I begin my morning chores."

"Don't be in such a hurry," said Tarantula. "Wouldn't you like to know what other people see when they look at your fine clothing?"

"How can I do that?" inquired the young warrior. Tarantula assured him it was an easy thing to do. "Let us exchange clothing," said the trickster. "That way you can look at me and see what your clothes look like." Without thinking, Swift-Runner did as he was asked, unaware that he was dealing with the wily trickster.

As soon as the two of them had exchanged outfits, Tarantula dived into a hole in the ground that led to his den. Swift-Runner was left standing outside with Tarantula's old clothes and his mouth wide open in surprise. Tarantula had tricked him. Sadly he returned home and told his father about Tarantula's deception. The two of them went to the village medicine man to ask advice. "Gather your friends," said the medicine man, "and together you can dig Tarantula out. Then you can get your clothes back."

Swift-Runner and his father did as the medicine man suggested. They gathered a group of warriors who tunneled deep into the earth but to no avail. Tarantula had dug his den very deep. Tired and disappointed, the warriors returned home. The next day the village leaders gathered to decide what to do about retrieving Swift-Runner's ceremonial outfit. They decided to hold a council about the matter.

At the council it was suggested that the leaders contact Kingfisher to help them catch the trickster. It was planned that Kingfisher would sit on the branch of a nearby tree and watch for Tarantula. He would attack the trickster when he crawled out of his den. Kingfisher agreed, and waited on a nearby stump. When the trickster came out he spied Kingfisher watching for him and quickly darted back into his den.

Village leaders had another meeting and decided to ask Eagle to help them catch Tarantula because Eagle had the sharpest eyes in the land. Surely he would be able to get Swift-Runner's clothes back from Tarantula. Eagle agreed to help the people. He flew high in a circle above Tarantula's den and waited for the trickster to appear. When Tarantula came out, Eagle dived down toward Tarantula, but the trickster was too fast for him. All Eagle caught was one of the plumes from the ceremonial outfit on Tarantula's head.

Everyone was very disappointed, especially Swift-Runner. He really wanted to have his ceremonial outfit back. Now the village leaders held a third meeting. This time they decided to invite Falcon to help them. After all, Falcon was the swiftest flying feathered creature in all the land. Falcon proudly agreed. He was eager to prove that he was equal to the sly trickster.

Falcon placed himself on the edge of a cliff near the trickster's den and waited. The sun was shining so brightly that Falcon was almost hidden in the direction that Tarantula would be looking. Everyone waited anxiously. Finally, the trickster emerged. Falcon left his perch like a shot, but Tarantula's speed saved him. He heard the sounds of Falcon's beating wings and with the speed of lightning retreated into his den. Still, it was a very close call for Tarantula. Falcon's sharp claws had scratched Tarantula's head, leaving deep wounds. The trickster retreated into his den to heal.

Once again, Swift-Runner was left without his ceremonial outfit. What could he do now? A fourth time the village leaders met to discuss the situation and came up with a new plan. They knew that Tarantula would eventually have to leave his den to get food. He could not last forever down there. They decided to out-wit the trickster.

One of Tarantula's favorite foods was deer meat so the village warriors asked several deer to help them with their plan. The deer stood against a white mountain so that their shadows appeared on the wall of the mountain. When Tarantula finally came out of his den to search for food he saw the shadows of the deer on the mountain wall, and his mouth watered. Although it was only shadows that he saw, he thought he was seeing real deer.

Cautiously the trickster looked around, and saw no one. He did not notice the warriors hidden in nearby trees. Tarantula shot some arrows at the deer from the doorway to his den, and it looked as though they had fallen to the ground. However, it was the real deer that dropped to the ground to make their shadows fall.

Tarantula was so excited that he sprang from his den and ran toward the place where the deer fell. As he did so, the warriors surrounded him. One of them blocked the doorway to Tarantula's den so he could not retreat. The rest of the warriors sprang on Tarantula and tore off Swift-Runner's clothing. This left Tarantula with no clothes on. He was so embarrassed he ran into the trees to hide.

It was a long time before Tarantula played another trick on anyone.

Learning Legends

Why Rabbits Have Short Tails
A Salish Legend

The animals of the earth used to have an annual race. Anyone who won a race was awarded the tail of an animal that lost the race. No one could run faster than Rabbit so he won a lot of races. He had the tail of Frog, and Bear, and his own beautiful long tail. Rabbit was surprised when Turtle agreed to challenge him.

"I will race with you," said Turtle, "but it should be a long race. I do not like short races. I do better in a long race."

Everyone laughed, and Rabbit made fun of Turtle's challenge. "Anyone can beat you," he said to Turtle. "You are the slowest animal in the whole forest." Turtle only smiled.

The day of the race was set. It was to be a long race as Turtle had requested. Everyone thought it would take Turtle a whole day to complete the race. At first the animals watched the race but it took a long time and they soon got bored. As the race began Rabbit took off at a fast speed and was soon out of sight. Turtle moved so slowly that some of the animals that were watching even fell asleep.

After a few minutes Rabbit slowed down and decided to take a nap while he waited for Turtle. While Rabbit was sleeping, Turtle passed him and continued slowly on his way. When Rabbit woke up he quickly ran past Turtle and then stopped for another nap. He did this four times. While he was on his fourth nap, Turtle passed him and crossed the finish line. Turtle was declared the winner.

Since Rabbit lost the race he had to give Turtle all the tails he had including Bear's tail, and Frog's tail. Rabbit cut off his own long tail so that only a little stubby part was left. Turtle looked at the tails and decided that Bear's tail was too bushy and Rabbit's tail was too long. He decided to take Frog's tail as his own. Rabbit was left with his short stubby tail which all rabbits have to this day.

Why Eagles are Bald
A Paiute Legend

All the animals and birds in the forest were disappointed with life. There were arguments and fights going on all the time. Everyone was unhappy with the way things were going but no one knew how to bring peace. Then one day someone suggested that there be a council of all the creatures in the forest to resolve the matter. Everyone should come to the council, all the animals and birds in the forest. Together they would decide a way to make peace in the forest.

Word about the meeting spread. One animal told another and each bird told others. Soon they all travelled to the place of the meeting. The bear, the wolf, and the fox came, and so did the eagle, the hawk, and the duck. Bees came, as well as small animals like the rabbit, the squirrel, and the prairie dog. Even crawling creatures attended the meeting.

Just before Eagle took off for the council meeting he saw his friend, Rattlesnake. "Are you going to the meeting?" Eagle asked Rattlesnake.

"No," said Rattlesnake. "The council is a long way from here and I cannot walk or run or fly. I can only crawl and that is a slow way to travel. There is no way I would make it to the council on time."

"Why don't you come with me," said Eagle. "Climb on my back and you can fly along with me." Rattlesnake liked the idea. He crawled aboard Eagle's back and wound himself around Eagle's neck. Then they were off.

As Eagle flew to the meeting place, Rattlesnake decided he would like to see where they were going, so he raised his head above Eagle's head and looked this way and that way as they flew. Each time he turned his head he shaved a few feathers off of the top of Eagle's head. He looked back and forth so often that by the time they arrived at the council location, Eagle's head was completely bald.

After a while some very short feathers grew back on Eagle's head but he has appeared to be bald-headed ever since.

By the way, the council meeting was successful and all the creatures at the meeting decided to live in peace.

Why Crows are Black
A Sioux Legend

Crows are black, but long ago they used to be white. In fact they were so light-colored that they seemed to be part of the sky. They were hard to see, and they were mischievous. When hunters went after the buffalo, crows would fly ahead of the hunters and warn the buffalo that the hunters were coming. Whenever the crows spotted hunters in the area where buffalo were grazing, they would fly overhead and go "Caw, caw, the hunters are coming." When the buffalo heard this they ran away. Soon the people had nothing to eat because the hunters were not able to shoot any buffalo.

The crows actions made the people upset. The people held a council with the hunters to see what could be done about the situation. The main problem was the leader of the crows who was an unusually large white bird. He was twice the size of the other crows but he could hardly be seen against the light sky. One wise old chief made the suggestion, "If we capture the leader of the crows and make him change his ways the others will follow. It is either that or the people will continue to go hungry." Everyone agreed.

The chief brought out a large old buffalo robe with the horns still attached to it. He put the robe on the back of a young hunter and told him to pretend he was one of the buffalo. "Sneak among the buffalo," he said, "and when the crows come to warn the buffalo, see if you can catch their leader." The young brave did as he was told.

Disguised as a buffalo, the young man joined the herd and acted just as they did. He moved like a buffalo, and pretended to eat grass. A group of hunters began to approach the buffalo, and the crows went into action. They began to make noises and warn the herd that the hunters were approaching.

Suddenly the big white crow who was the leader perched on the shoulder of one of the buffalo, and warned him, "Caw, caw, the hunters are coming." He did not know that he had landed on the shoulder of the young hunter who pretended to be one of the herd. The young brave reached out from under his buffalo robe and grabbed the feet of the crow leader. The crow struggled to get away but it was no use. The grip of the young hunter was firm and the crow leader was caught. The hunter tied the crow's feet to a heavy stone.

The people gathered in council. What was to be done about the crow leader? "Let's burn him," shouted one angry man. "He has done a great deal of damage to us. Many of us have very little food because of him. Let's really punish him."

A hot fire was burning at the center of the gathering. The angry man grabbed the large crow from his captor, and threw the bird into the fire. The crow tried hard to fly away but the heavy stone tied to his feet stopped him. He flailed his wings and managed to get out of the fire but all of his feathers were singed. The crow was no longer white. He was all black from the fire. The fire also burned the rope that held the stone to his feet and the stone fell away.

As he flew away slowly he cried out, "I'll never do it again; I'll never do it again!"

Since then crows' feathers have been black.

Why Buffalo Have Humps
An Anishinaubae Legend

Many moons ago when the earth was young, Buffalo did not have a big hump on his back. Buffalo loved to run across the prairie and feel the tall grasses beneath his feet. The fox always ran ahead of Buffalo to warn other animals that Buffalo was coming.

One day Buffalo started to run across the prairie to the place where birds make their nests on the ground. On this day Fox did not bother to warn the birds that Buffalo was coming and so Buffalo trampled on the bird's nests and destroyed them. The birds were very upset and told Nanabush (the trickster) what had happened.

Nanabush felt sorry for the birds and so he went to Buffalo and told him that he had done a very bad thing. Then he hit Buffalo with a long stick. Buffalo was afraid that Nanabush would hit him a second time so he humped up his shoulders in preparation for the blow.

Nanabush did not strike Buffalo a second time but told him this. "From now on you will stay this way. You will always have a hump on your shoulders because of what you have done. You should not have destroyed the birds' nests."

Then Nanabush turned to Fox and said, "You did not warn the birds that Buffalo was going to run across the prairie. You were unkind to the birds. From now on you will live in the cold ground."

Ever since that time Buffalo has had a hump on his back and Fox has made his home in the ground.

Why Porcupines Have Quills
A Chippewa Legend

Porcupines did not always have quills protruding from their bodies. In fact, they used to be very smooth skinned animals.

One day when Porcupine was walking in the woods Bear happened along and began to chase Porcupine. Porcupine was afraid that Bear would hurt him so he quickly climbed up into a tall tree. He felt safe in the tree because Bear could not reach him. Porcupine wished he had some means by which to keep Bear away. After a while Bear left.

A few days later Porcupine had an idea. He was hiding beneath a thorn bush and the needles were pricking his soft skin. Carefully he took some of the branches and tied them to his back. Then he went into the woods and waited for Bear to show up.

Soon Bear came by and saw Porcupine right on the path where he was walking. Bear sprang at Porcupine but Porcupine rolled himself into a ball. When Bear grabbed Porcupine he got badly scratched by the thorns that Porcupine had on his back. Bear did not know what to think so he ran away.

Nanabush (the trickster) was walking nearby and saw what happened. He felt sorry for Porcupine and took him back to the thorn bush. Nanabush stripped the bark off some of the branches. He put clay on Porcupine's back and stuck the bark with the thorns attached into the clay. Now Porcupine had a prickly back.

"Go into the woods," said Nanabush. "From now on you will have thorns on your body to protect you from your enemies."

Soon Wolf came along and saw Porcupine. Wolf attacked Porcupine by springing on top of him. To his surprise, Wolf got all scratched and quickly ran away. Neither Wolf nor Bear ever bothered Porcupine again.

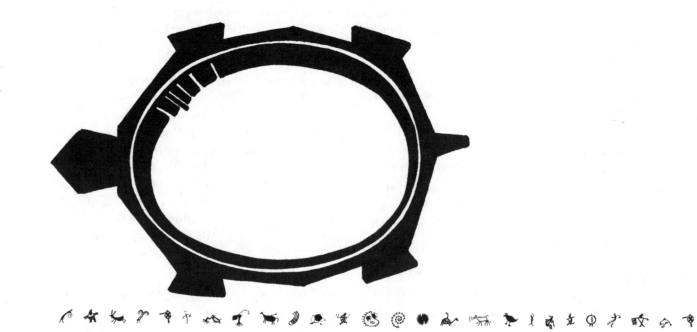

Why Turtles Hibernate
A Mik'Maq Legend

Among the Mik'maq people, you could always count on Turtle to tell a good story. When anyone got bored or lonely, they could always go to Turtle's house to hear a good tale. The only problem was that in the wintertime, Turtle always felt very cold, particularly during harsh winters when the cold would creep under his shell. Turtle's shell was hard, of course, and it generally protected him, but very cold winters were too much. When he was cold Turtle did not feel like telling stories.

Turtle's friends liked to hear his stories, so one fall day when the weather began to get cold, some of the geese decided to take him with them when they went south for the winter. After some thinking they figured out a way to transport Turtle. Turtle was asked to bite down hard on the middle of a long branch and two geese would each carry one of the ends of the branch in their bills. With Turtle biting hard on the branch the geese flew south. With Turtle along, they would be able to hear Turtle's stories every day.

Turtle found that the weather in the south did not suit him. It was too hot. He also missed his friends back home, and wanted to return there, in spite of the cold winters. Turtle decided to consult Glooscap about his problem. Glooscap suggested that Turtle go underground during the cold winter and sleep until spring. He could tell stories again when he awoke in spring. Sleeping all winter is called hibernation. Glooscap taught Turtle how to hibernate.

Turtle tried hibernating and he liked it. He also found that many of his other friends, like Bear, also hibernated. In spring when they all woke up they listened to Turtle's stories and everyone was happy.

Moral Legends

The Lesson of the Elm Tree
A Cherokee Legend

Good Eagle and Black Hawk were young boys who were very good friends. They played games together, climbed trees, and pretended to go on hunts. They longed for the day when they could go on a real hunt. Finally the day came. Good Eagle's father, Big Eagle, decided to take the two boys on their first hunt. Big Eagle was a respected hunter and warrior and the boys knew it was a real honor to be invited on a hunt with him.

Big Eagle decided that the boys should begin their lesson by hunting for small game. It was important that they learn to shoot well before hunting large animals. Today they would hunt rabbits for food. Good Eagle and Black Hawk were very excited.

They had not gone very far into the forest when the boys saw a rabbit and both of them let fly an arrow at exactly the same time. Both of their arrows struck the rabbit. Both boys shouted with delight. "I have killed my first rabbit." They began to argue about whose arrow had killed the rabbit and their voices got louder and louder. Finally Big Eagle spoke up. "I cannot tell whose arrow struck the rabbit first. Why don't we just say that you killed the rabbit together. One thing I know for certain. You are both as stubborn as elm trees."

"What does that mean?" both boys wanted to know. "In what way are we stubborn as elm trees?" Big Eagle refused to explain. "Come with me into the woods tomorrow and I will show you what I mean," he said.

The next day the three of them went into the woods and Big Eagle showed the boys the different kinds of trees that were in the forest. As he walked Big Eagle broke small branches off several trees. The boys followed him and also broke off branches. Finally they came to a tree with branches that would not break. The branches would only bend, all the way to the ground without breaking. Good Eagle and Black Hawk tried very hard to break the branches but they would not give.

"This is the elm tree," said Big Eagle. "Its branches will not break. It is a stubborn tree. This is what you boys were like yesterday when you argued about the rabbit. You were like elm trees."

The boys learned a valuable lesson. It is not always good to be stubborn.

Little Bear Earns a Feather
A Nez Percé Legend

Little Bear thought it was time for him to earn a feather. In Nez Percé culture it was believed that at a certain age young boys should earn a feather to show that they had become full-fledged warriors. Little Bear was very eager to earn his feather. To earn his feather he would have to do something very brave in hunting or in war to show that he could earn a feather and become a warrior.

Little Bear was worried because two summers ago his friends, Red Fox and Swift Deer had earned their feathers. Sometimes they walked in front of Little Bear's teepee to show off their feathers. Little Bear felt pressured to earn his feather too.

One day Little Bear's father, Big Bear, walked into the village with the body of a vicious mountain lion on his back. Little Bear was excited and asked his father what had happened. "You will have to wait until tonight's campfire," said Big Bear. "At that time I will tell the story."

Little Bear could hardly wait until evening because he wanted to hear all about his father's adventure with the mountain lion. Finally evening came and everyone gathered around the campfire to hear Big Bear's hunting story. Big Bear began unraveling the story slowly, and told how he had tracked a deer to shoot for his family's supper. Suddenly he heard a noise behind him. He turned quickly to see a mountain lion leaping right toward him. Just in time Big Bear fired an arrow and shot the huge cat in mid-air. He could not understand why the mountain lion had attacked him. Perhaps he had been too near the mountain lion's den or perhaps she had a cub in her den.

Little Bear's heart raced. Why couldn't he do a brave deed like his father and win his feather? Right then he decided to do something about it. Early the next morning he took his bow and arrows and a small bag of

food and left the village. He was careful to tell no one where he was going. He wanted to find the orphaned mountain lion's cub and bring it back to the village. He had an idea where to find the cub by listening carefully to his father's story.

After several hours of searching, Little Bear thought he heard the faint cry of a small animal. Perhaps it was the cub. The sound was close by. Little Bear followed the sound and there, not far away, he spied the mountain lion's cub. Little Bear moved slowly and quietly, but when he was just two steps way, the cub heard him and leaped away in fright. Little Bear also leaped, and pounced on the little animal, catching it by the scuff of its neck. He held the cub close and began gently scratching its neck. Soon it was purring in his arms. Little Bear took the cub in his arms and gently carried it to the village.

It was late in the afternoon when Little Bear arrived home and his parents had begun to worry. Little Bear's friends, Red Fox and Swift Deer met him near the entrance of the village. They were very curious about the cub he was carrying with him and wanted to know what had happened. Little Bear told his friends to wait until campfire time in the evening and he would tell his adventure.

That evening Little Bear felt proud of his achievement as the people gathered around the fire listened to his story. Everyone thought he was very brave to rescue the mountain lion cub because at any time Little Bear might have been attacked by a grown mountain lion. Big Bear was especially proud of his son.

Little Bear was awarded a feather because of his bravery. Now he was a full-fledged warrior.

Yellow Bird Learns a Lesson
A Pima Legend

There once was a young girl named Yellow Bird who lived with her parents in the southwestern United States. One day she told her mother that she wanted to pick berries, but her mother told her to wait until someone could go with her.

"It is too dangerous to pick berries by yourself," said Yellow Bird's mother. There are black bears around this time of year and they may attack you. Wait until someone can go with you."

Yellow Bird did not listen to her mother but instead took a basket and ran to the place where wild berries grow. On the way she met a big whirlwind that swept her up and put her on the top of a very high mountain. Yellow Bird was not hurt but she was badly frightened. She began calling for her mother but of course her mother could not hear her.

When Yellow Bird's mother discovered that her daughter was missing she went through the village looking for her. Unfortunately, no one had seen Yellow Bird so her mother became very upset. When Yellow Bird's father came home Yellow Bird was still missing. Quickly her father called his friends and organized a search party to look for his young daughter. He talked to his friend, a big black bird named Buzzard, and asked him to help as well.

"I will fly all over the land to see if I can find your daughter," said Buzzard. "Then I will come back and tell you what I have found."

Buzzard flew all over the land. He flew over rivers and lakes, and valleys and plains, but he did not find Yellow Bird. He came back to the village and told Yellow Bird's father that he had heard someone calling for help from on top of a very high mountain.

"I cannot fly that high," said Buzzard, "so I do not know who was calling out."

"That must have been my daughter calling out," said Yellow Bird's father. "We must find a way to rescue her." Quickly he and his friends travelled to the foot of the mountain where they heard Yellow Bird crying out. Immediately, they prepared to rescue her. First, they dug in the earth and planted some special gourd seeds. Then they said four prayers, and sang four songs and soon the seeds began to grow. A vine grew out of the ground and gradually it grew so tall that it reached the top of the mountain.

"Climb down the vine," Yellow Bird's father called to her. "It is a strong vine." Yellow Bird did as her father said, and soon reached the bottom of the mountain. She was very glad to see her father and be safely back on the ground.

"I will never disobey my mother again," she told her father. And she never did.

The Magic Hummingbird
A Hopi Legend

The Hopi people were worried. It had not rained for many months and their corn crop was drying up. Last year it had rained too much and the many plants had been washed away. The year before the frost came early and the corn crop was lost again. The Hopi people always stored plenty of corn for lean years, but now the supply was almost gone. What were the people to do?

Finally, the Hopi people decided to leave their traditional home on the mountain plateau and live elsewhere. Perhaps they would find a place where it would rain. Sadly they packed their belongings and said goodbye to the homes they had built. It was very hard to leave, but they knew that if they stayed, they might starve.

When the tribe left the plateau, three people were left behind, a boy named Red Fox, and his younger brother and sister. They had no mother or father to take them to the new village and the others seemed to forget about them.

Red Fox tried very hard to look after his brother and sister, but there was very little food. Each day Red Fox tried to find some root or berry bush with dried up fruit on it to feed them. He fashioned a toy bird for his sister from a sunflower stalk. She spent many happy hours playing with her new toy.

"Why not pretend your toy bird is real when you play with it?" Red Fox asked his sister. "Perhaps the Creator will see the bird and send food for it and for us."

His sister did as Red Fox suggested and often threw the sunflower bird into the air to make it look as though the bird could fly. One day when Red Fox came home from hunting for food he saw his sister crying.

"What is the matter, little one," he asked. "Where is the sunflower bird I made for you?"

To his surprise his sister remarked, "I threw the bird into the air and it flew away!" Then she started crying again.

Red Fox did not know what to do, but he told his sister he would look for the bird. He began to search everywhere, hoping the bird would show up.

Then he heard his sister call out. "Red Fox, come quickly, I just saw my sunflower bird fly by."

"Where did he fly to?" Red Fox asked. He was sure his little sister was playing make believe.

"He flew right into that hole in the stone wall," his sister insisted. "Please get him for me," she begged.

Red Fox asked his younger brother to put his hand into the hole in the wall while he went on looking for the sunflower bird. He was very surprised when his brother cried out.

"Red Fox, you must come and see. I have found a bin of corn. The hole in this wall is the opening to a great amount of stored corn. Now we will have plenty to eat."

Red Fox ran to his brother and put his hand into the hole. His brother was right. There was plenty of corn in the hidden bin. Now they would have food to eat for a long time. The three of them were very happy.

"See, I told you my bird came alive and it showed us the corn bin," the little sister exclaimed. Neither Red Fox nor his brother knew what to say. Then to their surprise a little hummingbird flew past them and into the hole that led to the secret bin of corn.

"Perhaps that was your toy sunflower bird," said Red Fox. "We may never be sure, but we will always be grateful."

Just then the tiny Hummingbird flew out of the hole and stopped in mid-air in front of the three of them. It beat its tiny wings very fast and remained in one spot for several minutes. It did this as if to say, yes, I am the sunflower toy bird.

Before long several people from the Hopi tribe came looking for the three children they had left behind. They were surprised to find that the children had plenty of food. In fact there was enough corn to feed the entire tribe for a long time. Soon the Hopi tribe returned to their traditional home and they have remained there to this day.

When Red Fox and his brother and his sister told the people the story of the sunflower bird that turned into a hummingbird they were very grateful. Since then the hummingbird has been very special to the Hopi people.

The Bow Maker
An Apache Legend

There was a very poor grandmother in an Apache village who had many grandchildren to look after. Often there was very little to eat in the house. The oldest of her grandchildren was a shy boy who had very few friends. Everyone teased him and called him names. Mostly they called him Poor Boy because his grandmother did not have many things.

Poor Boy worked hard to help his grandmother take care of their home. He collected firewood and took care of his younger brothers and sisters. He tried to go hunting with the men of the village but they said he was too young.

One day Poor Boy had an idea. He learned that an old hunter named Mountain Man was an excellent bow maker. Bows and arrows were very important to hunters and it was necessary to have a very good bow for hunting. Mountain Man made the best bows in the village.

One day Poor Boy asked Mountain Man if he would teach him how to make bows. To his surprise Mountain Man said he would do so. "I have been looking for someone to learn the trade," said Mountain Man. "I am an old man and someone will soon have to take my job."

Poor Boy was so excited that he ran all the way home to share the news with his grandmother. When he arrived home he was so out of breath that his grandmother could not understand a word he was saying.

"Slow down, Poor Boy," the grandmother said. "Just what are you trying to tell me?"

Poor Boy caught his breath. "Mountain Man said he would teach me how to make bows," he gasped. "Then I will have a trade and will be able to make useful things."

"You do many useful things around here," Poor Boy's grandmother told him. "I am glad that you will learn how to make bows, but I am also grateful for your help at home." She patted Poor Boy on the shoulder and he ran off to do chores.

Soon Poor Boy went to work with Mountain Man and he quickly learned how to make excellent bows. Mountain Man always used cedar wood for his bows although most warriors used other kinds of wood. It took a lot longer to make bows with cedar. Poor Boy learned how to steam cedar so it would bend. He also learned how to scrape the bow with a sharp stone and soak bands of sinew in water to make bowstrings. It was very hard work but Poor Boy was an eager student.

When he was fourteen years old Poor Boy was allowed to go on his first hunt with the men. Early in the morning the hunting party got on their horses and rode to find a buffalo herd. Shortly after they left the village they spotted a buffalo herd. Everyone in the hunting party rode toward the animals. Poor Boy was the first to bring down a buffalo with his bow and arrow and everyone was greatly surprised.

"How could a young boy shoot such a magnificent animal so quickly?" one of the warriors wanted to know. The hunters examined Poor Boy's bow and were amazed at its beauty and admired the skill with which it was made.

"How did you learn to make such a beautiful bow?" they all asked.

Poor Boy was very proud. This was the moment he had been waiting for. "Mountain Man taught me how to make bows," he said. "It takes a long time to make a good bow and we only make them out of cedar wood."

Every one wanted Poor Boy to make a bow for them. "I want one just like yours," one hunter said, and Poor Boy promised to make one for him. In fact, it wasn't long after that Poor Boy became known as Man-who-makes-bows. The hunters called him Bow Man for short.

Bow Man, his grandmother, and his brothers and sisters never went hungry again.

The Lazy Ravens
A Haida Legend

The Haida people used to be very kind to ravens. Whenever they caught fish the people fishing would share them with the ravens. The big black croaking birds would follow the fishing boats and beg for food and the fishermen would give them some.

As time went on, however, the ravens got lazy and stopped following the fishermen. Instead they went directly to the fishermen's nets and stole fish from them. This angered the fishermen who told the ravens they would not feed them any longer.

"We were quite happy to share our fish with you," they told the ravens, but you went too far when you started stealing them out of our nets."

The fishermen's words made the ravens very angry and they began to threaten the fishermen. "The next time the fish begin their run up the river, we'll take them all," the ravens said. "Then you will have no fish at all."

The Haida fishermen began to worry. They needed the fish run. The fish provided them with food as well as oil for cooking and light. On the other hand, what could a flock of ravens do? How could they catch all the fish? The fishermen decided to go back to their fishing.

Late one night the voice of Raven, the trickster, was heard in the Haida camp. "Just wait until the moon comes out tonight. Something is going to happen. The ravens might catch all the fish and there will be none left for you."

Again the fishermen were worried. They knew all about Raven's tricks so they had reason to be concerned. They wondered what he was up to.

Soon the moon came up and shone brightly across the water. For an hour nothing happened. Then Raven spoke again. "I am going to steal the moon," he warned the Haida fishermen. "Then you will no longer be able to fish at night."

At first the fishermen thought Raven was joking. How could anyone steal the moon? Some of them laughed out loud. But wait, this was Raven the trickster. He could do very unpleasant things.

Suddenly it got very dark. Everyone looked around but they could no longer see the moon. Raven had indeed stolen the moon. Everyone began to beg Raven to bring the moon back.

"If you promise to feed the ravens, I will bring back the moon," said Raven. "You must keep your promise. From now on, whenever you go fishing and the ravens ask you to share your catch, you must do so. This is the nature of sharing."

The Haida promised to do as Raven asked. They said they would share their fish with the ravens. Even today, the Haida fishermen on the Queen Charlotte Islands always toss a bit of fish to any raven who asks for it.

The Grateful Wolf
A Tsimshian Legend

When the weather turned cold a band of Tsimshian Indians decided to move further south on the British Columbia west coast. When they arrived at their destination, they made camp, ate supper, and turned in for the night. The next morning when they awoke they saw a very large wolf sitting at their campfire. The wolf looked very thin. One of the warriors spoke to Wolf but he did not answer.

"Perhaps Wolf is hungry," said one of the women. "He looks very thin. Why don't we give him some food?"

"That is a good idea," said the band chief, so some of the women prepared some deer meat and gave it to Wolf. To everyone's surprise, Wolf refused to eat the meat. He just sat and stared into the fire. After a while the people began to walk around Wolf and make comments. "Maybe Wolf is sick," said one observer. "I never saw a wolf who would not eat anything that was placed in front of him."

Finally one brave warrior thought there must be something seriously wrong with Wolf so he took a look down Wolf's throat. Sure enough, a large fish-hook was lodged in the wolf's throat so he could neither talk nor eat. Slowly he reached inside the wolf's mouth and worked the hook loose until he could remove it. Immediately Wolf began to talk.

"You are very kind people," said Wolf. "You have saved my life. Please let me stay with you a little while until my strength is back. Then I will help you in any way I can. I will always be grateful to you." The people agreed. They provided food for Wolf and after a few days he was on his way. No one expected to hear from him again. After all, there was not anything that a wolf could do for people.

Some time passed, and winter came. Game was scarce, and there were few fish to catch. The people began to grow hungry and every day hungry children's cries could be heard in the camp. Winter ended and there was no food left to eat. No one knew what to do. The people began to pray to the Creator for food.

One day Wolf's shadow fell across the door of the chief's lodge. He looked strong and healthy. "Hello there," Wolf called. "I know you are in trouble so I came to help." Everyone stared at Wolf. Where had he come from? The village hunters looked at each other questioningly then asked Wolf. "Where can you find food when we have tried so hard and found none?"

"Why not trust me?" said Wolf. "You helped me before and now it is my turn to help you." Wolf's words made sense. The people had helped him. Perhaps he wanted to return the favor.

Several hunters followed Wolf into the forest. Although it was spring, there were places where the snow was still deep. The hungry hunters had to stop several times to rest. They were too weak to follow the strong wolf. Wolf always waited for them until they were able to travel again.

Suddenly in a clearing in the forest a small herd of caribou mysteriously appeared. Quickly the hunters placed arrows to their bows and shot. The arrows struck the caribou and the men quickly cut up and prepared the meat to eat. Wolf watched the hungry men go about their work and then disappeared into the forest. The hunters tried to thank him just before he left, but all he would say was, "We are all brothers and we must help one another."

When the men returned to their camp with the meat everyone was very grateful to Wolf. All the people wanted to thank Wolf but he was nowhere to be found. To show their gratitude, the village carver carved the figure of Wolf onto their next totem pole.

The Happy Duck
An Ojibway Legend

There was once a very happy duck. No one knew why Duck was so happy, and nothing seemed to take away his happiness. Duck was simply happy.

One day North Wind heard about Duck and decided to see if there was anything he could do to make Duck less happy. North Wind decided to use his powers to bother Duck. The next day when Duck went fishing, North Wind froze the lake which made it difficult for Duck to catch fish. Duck had to cut a hole in the ice much deeper than usual but he still managed to catch a few fish. He went home singing.

North Wind decided to try again. He went to Duck's lodge and knocked on the door. Duck heard North Wind and decided not to answer the door. North Wind blew his coldest blast under the door of the lodge, but Duck still would not answer. Finally North Wind blew the door open, went inside, and sat down beside Duck. Duck pretended not to see him. He just went on singing.

Duck stirred up the flames in his fireplace and the fire burned brightly. Soon North Wind began to get very warm. North Wind blew cold air on the fire but it was too hot even for him to cool. Quickly, he backed away from the fire but still the frost on his white beard began to melt. North Wind knew if he did not get out of Duck's lodge he would melt away. Quickly North Wind moved towards the door while Duck kept on singing.

The next day North Wind made the ice on the lake even thicker so Duck would not be able to go fishing. Duck managed to find a breathing hole left by a seal and still caught a few fish. Then he went home singing.

"I give up," said North Wind. He never bothered Duck again and Duck went right on being happy.

About the Authors

John W. Friesen, Ph.D., D.Min., D.R.S., is a Professor in the Graduate Division of Educational Research at the University of Calgary where he teaches courses in Aboriginal history and education. He is an ordained minister with the All Native Circle Conference of the United Church of Canada, the recipient of three eagle feathers, and author of more than 40 books including the following Detselig titles.

Schools With A Purpose, 1983;

The Cultural Maze: Complex Questions on Native Destiny in Western Canada, 1991;

When Cultures Clash: Case Studies in Multiculturalism, 1993;

Pick One: A User-Friendly Guide to Religion, 1995;

Rediscovering the First Nations of Canada, 1997;

Sayings of the Elders: An Anthology of First Nations' Wisdom, 1998;

First Nations of the Plains: Creative, Adaptable and Enduring, 1999;

Legends of the Elders, 2000;

Aboriginal Spirituality and Biblical Theology: Closer Than You Think, 2000;

In Defense of Public Schools in North America (co-author), 2001;

Aboriginal Education in Canada: A Plea for Integration (co-author), 2002;

More Legends of the Elders (co-author), 2004; and,

We Are Included!: The Métis People of Canada Realize Riel's Vision (co-author), 2004.

Virginia Lyons Friesen, Ph.D., is a Sessional Instructor in the Faculty of Communication and Culture at the University of Calgary. An Early Childhood Education specialist, she holds a certificate in counseling from the Institute of Pastoral Counseling in Akron, Ohio. She served as Director of Christian Education with the Morley United Church on the Stoney (Nakoda Sioux) Indian Reserve from 1988 to 2001.

She has presented papers at learned conferences and is co-author of:

Grade Expectations: A Multicultural Handbook for Teachers (Alberta Teachers' Association, 1995);

In Defense of Public Schools in North America (Detselig, 2001);

Aboriginal Education in Canada: A Plea for Integration (Detselig, 2002);

More Legends of the Elders (Detselig, 2004);

The Palgrave Companion to North American Utopias. (Palgrave Macmillan, 2004); and,

We Are Included!: The Métis People of Canada Realize Riel's Vision (Detselig, 2004).